A New Tomorrow

A New Tomorrow

Activating Your Vision for a Better World

Ari Gronich

Copyright © 2019 Ari Gronich

All rights reserved. No part of this book may be reproduced or transmitted in any form or by any means without written permission of the publisher, except in the case of brief quotations embedded in critical articles and reviews.

This material has been written and published solely for educational purposes. The author and the publisher shall have neither liability nor responsibility to any person or entity with respect to any loss, damage, or injury caused or alleged to be caused directly or indirectly by the information contained in this book.

The author of this book does not dispense medical advice or prescribe the use of any technique as a form of treatment for physical, emotional, or medical problems without the advice of a physician, either directly or indirectly. The intent of the author is only to offer information of a general nature to help the reader in the quest for well-being. In the event the reader uses any of the information in this book for self or others, which is a constitutional right, the author and the publisher assume no responsibility for the actions of the reader.

Statements made in this book have not been evaluated by the Food and Drug Administration. This book and its contents are not intended to diagnose, treat, or cure any infection, injury, or illness, or prevent any disease. Results vary and each person's experience is unique.

Statements made and opinions expressed in this publication are those of the author and do not necessarily reflect the views of the publisher or indicate an endorsement by the publisher.

ISBN: 978-1-945446-71-9

This book is dedicated to the memory of Buckminster Fuller and all he contributed to the future of society.

Contents

Acknowledgments 9
Introduction 11

CHAPTER ONE
  Mindset, Critical Thinking, And A 360-Degree
  Point Of View 15
    The Butterfly Effect 15
    Finding The Root 23
    What Are Your Options? 33

CHAPTER TWO
  The Current State Of
    Healthcare And Medicine 43
      Western Medicine 43
      Single-Layer Thinking 51
      Insular Practice 57

CHAPTER THREE
  Why I Do What I Do 67
    My Pain 67
    My Process 76
    My Results 83

CHAPTER FOUR
  The Future Of Medicine   91
    Do We Enhance The System
      Or Start Over?   91
    Health Is Not About Medical Care   95
    Infrastructure And Healthcare   101

CHAPTER FIVE
  The Future Of Society   107
    Plan For The Future
      Or Plan For The Present?   107
    Using Technology To Bring Us
      Back To Nature   113
    The Power Of Change   120

Conclusion   127
Next Steps   129
About The Author   131

Acknowledgments

*For all things blessed, there is the bitter
that makes the sweet so much better.*

I want to thank my family and friends who have forever shaped the way that I see the world.

My mom and dad, who have never left my side, even when they probably should have.

My wife, who suffers the real me—good, bad, and ugly—and still looks at me with loving eyes.

My kids, who light my life and give me a purpose for becoming better inside myself.

All the mentors over the years who have helped move me from the pits of despair to the highest stars.

Lastly, I acknowledge the dreamers who dare to lift themselves beyond the pain and give the greatest of treasures to those they touch.

Introduction

This book is about the future. It is about how we see ourselves and how we see our contribution to society. It is about how we can activate ourselves to live passionately, and while doing so, how we can enhance the health, wealth, and nature of society so we can *all* live happy and fulfilled lives.

My name is Ari Gronich. I have been a sport and rehab therapist and a functional medicine consultant for nearly twenty-five years. I am an innovator. I am an outside-of-the-box thinker, and I am a motivator. I am passionate about what my mind creates and about seeing those creations come to fruition. And I am a healer.

I want to heal the world, and the only way I can do that is with you. I have a passion for the transformation of the current norms in society. I have faith that with critical thinking, a good mindset, excitement about possibilities, and a willingness to go through fear and anxiety, we can all create what we want.

I would like to see society change for the better, and that is why I have written this book. I have been activated to try to create the society I want to see in the future, and this book has become an important part of my vision.

What transforms me and excites me is seeing modern health inventions — or any of the genius creations that we as a society create. Back in the day, this creativity was provided by people like Leonardo da Vinci. Today it comes from people like Elon Musk.

And tomorrow, it will be you.

I would like to know that I helped you create the future that you want. It is my hope that reading this book will inspire you to become activated to pursue your path with passion and purpose. I can't wait to hear about and experience what you create in this world.

I suggest you read this book with a journal next to you. As you read, you may find that you come up with ideas for what you want to create. You might come up with insights and realizations about your life. You might come up with ideas about your possible contributions, about how you want to transform yourself and society.

If you are in the field of medicine and health, you will want to write down the things you can do to make changes you know will benefit your patients and improve health in your communities. You can use this book as a workbook and activate yourself through journaling. Write down what you are passionate about as you read. Write down what strikes you as something that you would like to see happen or you would like to be a part of. Then, you can begin to create an action plan to accomplish those changes.

This book was designed to help you begin this process. I hope that it will become a guide for your life and will help you shift and transform into the person you want to become. I hope it will help you cultivate faith, purpose, and passion in your life — as well as a higher purpose for the society that you can change — and the legacy you can leave.

CHAPTER ONE

―――――――――

Mindset, Critical Thinking, and a 360-Degree Point of View

THE BUTTERFLY EFFECT

A butterfly flaps its wings on a tranquil sunny morning.

As a result, a storm rages halfway across the globe.

Cause and effect: The smallest of movements can create the largest of changes. If this *butterfly effect* postulation is true, that everything is interconnected and interwoven with everything else, then all things must have an origin. Therefore, whatever goals you have, whatever problems you want to solve, you must trace the issues back to the beginning to find the root causes.

Decisions Have Effects

A lack of critical thinking, including a lack of consideration for this butterfly effect, was at the helm of many failures in history, including the collapse of the Roman Empire.

A society devoid of critical thinking is a civilization on the brink of collapse.

The decisions we make today ripple out into the world and create consequences. If the last seventy years have taught us anything, it is that when we obstruct and divert the natural order, we cause chaotic results.

This is what happens when agriculture turns to planting big mono-crops rather than growing a diversity of foods and rotating the cycles. It is what happens when beneficial natural plant medicines are transformed into pharmaceutical drugs with damaging side effects. Science is often too much about isolating compounds, rather than incorporating and enhancing them in a natural manner. When we target and isolate nutrients into their chemical and molecular parts — as extracts — we lose the cofactors that create synergy within the natural environment of that plant.

In addition, these isolation techniques can create dangerous chemicals from fairly harmless natural substances. A plant like valerian root, for instance, which has been used in its natural state to combat anxiety disorders and other stress-related issues, can be turned into valium. This powerful drug has its origins in the natural plant, but when isolated and turned into a pharmaceutical, it comes with additional side effects that can be harmful. These negative side effects are a direct result of isolating instead of incorporating and synergizing.

The Effects on Medicine

In anyone's health journey, we can see markers along the way—signs or symptoms—that are related to the decisions we have made. Having a heart attack, for example, may be related to eating at fast food restaurants, working eighty hours a week, and being filled with stress and worry.

We all know that the decisions we make are directly related to our subsequent experiences. We can trace the relationships even farther back by looking at the decisions that were made *before* we made our decisions.

Let me give you an example. At some point in your life, you may make the decision to *eat healthy* to improve your health. To accomplish this, you select a diet that you consider healthy, like a low-fat diet that follows the United States Department of Agriculture (USDA) Standard American Diet (SAD) guidelines.

What happens if you make what you think is a healthy choice but it does not improve your health at all? What do you do when your decision gets you subpar results? It's time to look back even farther. It's time to ask some good questions and find the root cause of the problem.

In this case, you might ask:

- *Why were these dietary guidelines ineffective?*
- *How did the USDA come up with the Standard American Diet guidelines?*
- *What were the actions that happened prior to the USDA creating the guidelines that have proven to be ineffective?*
- *What happened before that?*
- *And, what happened before that?*

Do you understand where I am headed with this?

Before we can genuinely solve a problem, we must ask the questions that enable us to trace the root causes of the problem.

In our society, we tend to seek out quick-fix remedies, especially when it comes to health problems. We seek a prescription instead of seeking out the root causes of illness. Many of us, unfortunately, are not trained to think critically or to use deductive reasoning, and as such, we focus on creating treatments for disease symptoms rather than looking for cures for disease origins. To find root causes, we must trace the issues back to their beginnings.

In medicine, in the study of basic anatomy and physiology, we are taught that the body is an incredible healing machine, and it is in a continuous search for and creation of *homeostasis*. Homeostasis, according to the Oxford Dictionary, is *the tendency toward a relatively stable equilibrium between interdependent elements, especially as maintained by physiological processes.*

To put this in layman's terms: *Your body is always seeking balance.*

It is our job to give our bodies what they need to accomplish their job. If we do this successfully, organ by organ and process by process, the result will be a healthy body.

Can't we expand this strategy to determine how to create a healthy society?

If we consider every aspect of life and living that could affect these bio-systems we call bodies, then how we develop our communities and our society will reflect the principles by which nature has intended us to live. This way of thinking has its own butterfly effect that can expand into all aspects of how we live and interact with each other and the world around us.

The Effects on Society

Society benefits from balance. When we work within the laws of nature, we can learn how to create technology that is supportive of nature and of balance. When we think in this manner on a concrete level, we can create cities and communities that reflect this ideal.

Here are some examples:

- Our roads, buildings, and infrastructure can be designed in way that adds to health and vitality.

- We have the ability to develop transportation systems that are impact-neutral on the environment and, in some cases, actually nurture it.

- Company campuses can include gardens that produce fresh organic food, which help nurture employees, keeping them alert, productive, and energetic.

- Safe walking paths lined with fruit trees are a great way to encourage people to exercise and get some *fast food* on the go.

- Shielding technologies that help cut the electromagnetic storm have a tangible effect on our body stress levels and in turn, on our immune systems and our ability to stay healthy.

- Sewage systems that not only take the waste away from the center of the city, but also recycle the waste into biofuels, fertilizers, and other usable commodities perpetuate growth of technology and sustainable resources at the same time.

In other words, if we think about the consequences of our actions all the way down the timeline, we can develop a system and a society that operate under optimal standards for the health of all nature. Remember, every system that has ever been created was simply made up by us. If we can make it up, we can choose to create a more optimal system and let the failing system have its demise.

This idea is in alignment with natural principles, as well as Buddhist teachings, which tell us that destruction can lead to a healthy rebirth. We do not need to aim to destroy the old sub-optimal way of doing things; we simply create new and more optimized ways to improve the overall health of society. Society can thrive with this natural progressive way of thinking.

A butterfly effect will also be demonstrated by these kinds of incremental changes. A linked series of action-to-result events becomes like a set of dominos set up for structural falling. We set the system up and then watch it fall while enjoying all aspects of the journey from the building to the falling.

Consider all the possibilities. Following this line of thinking, we can build communities that are designed to encourage mobility, with walking paths through beautiful gardens in bright colors, with vegetables and fruit growing everywhere. We can install water treatment plants that clean the water and remove contaminants without the use of toxic chemicals and institute air pollution policies that support clean air initiatives. We can allow the use of newer technologies whenever they are available rather than when the market share lets them be distributed for financial gain.

One of the things that we know about nature and the environment is that it can change within a moment's notice. We've all had those days at the beach when we're frolicking in the sun one minute and running to the car in a rainstorm the next—just to see the sun coming back out as soon as we're leaving the parking lot. Since we are all aware of the changeable nature of our environment, we can design systems that are modular and easily upgradeable, and this will enable us to move our projects forward quickly as we implement the changes that support a natural society.

Part of looking ahead is being able to see the multiple possibilities that the butterfly effect can produce. It does not have to be a hurricane across the world from the butterfly's wings; it could be a soft breeze on a hot day. Knowing the many possibilities will help us plan for contingencies so that we will be ready for whatever comes.

FINDING THE ROOT

As we look forward in planning the ideal, it is imperative that we look back at the causes of what we are now experiencing. Studying our history can help illustrate this process.

For example, what was the cause of the plague? What were the causes of polio, scurvy, and other diseases?

In answering these questions, remember that you don't just want to look at the bacterial or viral culprits, but also at the *root causes* of the spread of disease. If we look back at our history, we can discover these root causes, and in addition, we may well be inspired by the solutions that our ancestors came up with to remove those issues from their societies.

Breaking Down Symptoms to Their Origins

The Romans had some great answers to disease and other problems that were plaguing their society. First, they built aqueducts and reservoirs to store and bring quality water to the communities. They devised systems to bring in clean water for the bathhouses and for cooking. At the same time, they installed sewer systems to remove waste. Many of the diseases that they were suffering from were specifically due to the bacteria and bugs that hang out with waste. The Romans broke the symptoms down to the root causes. When they fixed those root causes, the problems were greatly reduced.

The Chinese broke down symptoms to the organ level. They would then break the function of each organ down to energy and emotional levels. They identified complex networks of points on the body that they found would have profound effects on the organs and on the health of the body. They created *acupuncture* to help acute situations as well as support chronic imbalances. The Chinese related organs to function and function to emotion, and they used this information to identify ways to remedy problems.

For example, if the liver is responsible for processing the poop and the liver is toxic, this imbalance may result in trouble letting go, as in constipation. Alternatively, the liver's inability to work properly may cause letting go without being able to process, and that may result in diarrhea. Chinese medicine will often focus on specific acupuncture points, along with particular herbs, roots, and foods that would support the troubled organ.

These Chinese practitioners were ahead of the times in the approach they took; however, they were not looking at the environmental factors that cause the illness in the first place. The methods they used focused on treating symptoms instead of treating root causes. If we are going to create thriving societies, we must focus on root causes and address them first. This is equivalent to chopping an onion in half and pulling out the core, rather than peeling the onion layer by layer.

Here is the great news: This process does not need to be painful. If society makes a commitment to correcting the root causes, if we focus on developing a mindset that supports critical thinking and deductive reasoning, we have a chance to create something that simply replaces the current system in a natural way.

It is not about forcing the current system out. That would cause resistance and conflict. It is about planned, intentional release of new communities surrounding the current communities. We can create places that people *want* to move into. As early adopters migrate to these intentional communities, the voids left in current communities naturally create an incentive for the demolishing and rebuilding of these places with a new way of thinking.

The results evidenced and experienced in one place will cause other places to pop up. Before you know it, we will have rebuilt the world from the origins up to create symptoms of joy, health, and happiness instead of stress, sickness, and depression.

The Rat Race Is the Alternative

If we, as a society, do not embrace this way of thinking and continue according to our current modus operandi, we are doomed to repeat history. We are condemned to the rat race in which our society finds itself. Most people right now truly believe that there is no hope.

Too many of our days consist of the same rat-race schedule:

Wake up
Shower
Eat
Kiss kids and spouse — or many don't even do that anymore
Get in the car and drive to work
Texting, texting, texting
Work, which often consists of maybe three productive hours out of an eight-hour-day, the remainder of hours in a fog
Texting some more
Drive home
Eat dinner
Sit on the couch and watch television
Go to bed
Rinse and repeat every weekday

After the week is over, the weekends are for all the chores you didn't get done during the week. Maybe you have a day to chill with family before doing it again. And again. And again. For the next forty years — unless you are laid off and have a few years in which you're trying to find another job where you can do the same thing.

Huh, that was a long paragraph just to write. I feel like the rat race took me over for a second. I need to pause for a moment.

Okay. I am back.

Take a moment and see how this scenario makes you feel. You can feel your soul being sucked out of you, from just reading about this day.

How does it make your body feel? I know I want a deep breath or two.

How many of you stop to breathe?

Take a second to ask yourself these questions:

- *How do I want to feel living my life?*
- *Whom do I want to be in my life?*
- *What kind of example or legacy do I want to leave my kids?*
- *If I could construct my ideal life, what would it look like?*

If these questions make you think and wonder, ask them often. Spend some time to reverse-engineer the life you want.

If these questions make you uncomfortable and feel like brand-new concepts to you, you may want to spend a lot of time with the questions. If you don't, you will remain spinning on the wheel in your personal rat race.

Natural Solutions and the Speed of Shift

What is beautiful about how nature works is that once we decide to let nature flow through us, we can move remarkably fast. The *speed of shift* is unbelievable; the manifestation when you are in the flow is instantaneous.

Have you ever thought of someone and not two minutes later, that person calls you on the phone or you bump into them in the store?

We are amazing creators, we humans. It is one of the gifts we have been given that separates us from the rest of the other animal kingdom. We can create towers from our minds, rocket ships off to the moon, submarines that let us cruise and explore the oceans, and planes that let us travel through the air.

We are incredible at manifesting, and when we begin to match nature, we learn that everything flows easily.

Did you know that, in nature, if there is something poisonous near you, there is a cure for that poison close by?

There is a natural solution for every problem in nature. Illness and disease in the future will be much smaller problems when we understand nature. We will learn how to see the root causes and when we do, we can implement the solutions quickly and easily. Instead of battling microbes in a way that causes the development of super-strains of viruses, bacteria, and parasites, we can find ways to discourage their presence. We can develop our societies and communities in ways that mitigate exposure to disease-causing microbes by simply making it inherently inhospitable for them to coexist with us.

When we take the time to think out natural solutions, the results are often much better than those we might find from manmade solutions. A good example is the battle in Florida against mosquitoes. Rather than working with natural solutions, the strategy has been to drive through communities spraying the streets and air with pesticides and other chemical concoctions. The people in these communities were also affected because they were breathing air and eating foods that were contaminated with these chemicals. Lastly, although the pesticides did kill some mosquitoes, many developed immunities to the chemicals; thus, mosquitoes are still rampant in Florida.

Bats and dragonflies are great mosquito eaters. A natural solution for the mosquito problem could be strategically placed bat houses that take into consideration the human population, the mosquito population, and the bat population. A natural solution that is well thought out will have a low impact on the environment. It will also have more beneficial effects than side effects. Following a chain of thought like this is what allows things to happen at the speed of shift.

Consider the impact of stress on our population. We know that stress-related diseases in people are common. In fact, in the United States, stress is related to the top six causes of death and illness: heart disease, cancer, lung ailments, accidents, cirrhosis of the liver, and suicide, according to a 2014 Miami Herald article.[1] It is clear that stress reduction should be part of creating healthy lives.

The first step is asking questions like:

- How does stress impact health?
- What are the root causes of stress?
- What is a natural solution to address this problem in our society?

---

1 Hartz-Seeley, Deborah S. "Chronic stress is linked to the six leading causes of death." Miami Herald. 21 March 2014. miamiherald.com/living/article1961770.html

- How can we create lives that lessen heavy stressors and increase relaxation, rejuvenation, and fun?
- What stress-reducing treatment techniques can enable people to heal faster?
- How would these approaches impact our physical health, our mental health, and our quality of life?
- How would this approach affect the way we treat each other in our society?

Imagine what would happen if you went to the doctor for heart palpitations and got prescribed a week of lying on the beach and receiving massages and pampering, instead of a set of drugs and procedures. How much more productive would you be? How much more friendly would our neighbors and fellow citizens be?

Looking for root causes involves more than looking at your own personal behaviors and lifestyle, although these are great starting points. Finding the root requires looking at all the environmental and social symptoms as well, until the issue is traced back to the beginning.

When you think this way, you will begin to shape your experiences, and you cannot help but activate yourself, as well as others. When you begin to shift, those near you will want to be around you; they will want to become like you. People can see the alteration from what was to what is, and they will naturally want to follow. This can move an entire society in a new direction.

For those who truly understand these principles, now is the time to gather and begin shifting and changing. Now is the time to organize, plan, and create. For those who can't see the shift coming, remember that rat race!

WHAT ARE YOUR OPTIONS?

The first step to any beginning is in the making of a decision to create an experience:

- *I choose to leave my house today . . .*
- *I choose to go to the beach today . . .*
- *I choose to work at what I am passionate about and want to wake up and get out of bed for . . .*
- *I choose to do what I have always done . . .*

Start by asking yourself these questions: *What are my options today? What do I want to create today?*

Then wait for the infinite list of possibilities to arise.

Consider the possibilities, and make the decision that feels best in the moment. For me, when I do this consistently, I find that I am more prosperous, healthy, and joyful. Interestingly, I am also more productive. It is funny how creating my passion as my work means that very often my decisions are to work, create, and be productive.

The people close to you will also benefit. When you feel better inside, when you feel fulfilled, you will treat family and friends in a more loving and kind way. In addition, as others watch you lead a fulfilling life, they will be inspired to follow your lead and find their own fulfillment. Happiness is contagious.

Gathering Your Resources

After deciding to live and create from your passion, there is more work to be done. Gathering your resources together, including key people, is a great beginning.

Once you are clear as to what you want and about who and what needs to be a part of the process, it will become easier to make plans. Spend some time thinking carefully about what you will need to proceed.

For example, if your passion is to be a carpenter, what resources might you need? A wood supplier, some equipment, a facility, designers?

If your passion is to clean up the environment, what might you need? Engineers, test areas, scientific studies, technology, volunteers, employees, advocates, activists, plans and designs for something new and different, or solutions that are readily implementable? You get the idea.

Once you identify all the resources that you need, you can gather those resources and share your passion. Create a company, lobby your local politicians, engage the community, and look for grant money, loans, and other funding.

Nature supplies a solution to every problem and challenge. When your mindset is always looking for the causes, you will inherently begin to develop solutions. Your resources will become your immune system and will keep your dreams healthy and moving forward. When people create from this solution-oriented position, the side effects become fewer and the benefits rise. Our society shifts, our communities grow together, and we live healthier lives.

Asking Leading and Critical Questions

Beginning with questions is a powerful way to start any solution-oriented conversation. Asking leading and critical questions is the way to dig deep into the solutions and possibly to find other hidden consequences that may happen because of your proposed decisions.

For example, suppose you are considering electric vehicles as a solution to clean air.

Here are some critical questions you might ask:

- How much pollution is caused by the mining, transportation, manufacturing, and assembly of the raw materials that it takes to create the batteries that store the electricity to run the car?

- What are the unintended consequences of displacing workers in the other industries that support the current oil and coal industries?

- How can we train, educate, and support those people in finding new jobs so they would be passionate about the new technology or a new industry all together?

Be willing to criticize your plan and take suggestions from other experts. This is especially vital in the medical and holistic health industry as there have been many conflicts between different disciplines in these fields, due to a lack of understanding, a lack of knowledge, or outright disagreements regarding methods. Knowing this in advance and being able to place a critical eye on yourself is what will help you find solutions now rather than when disaster strikes.

You can avoid a lot of pain and mistakes by asking commonsense, critical, and leading questions. Use your resources to help you create balance. Putting together a group of diverse people will give you the benefit of different perspectives. They may be able to see things that you are blind to and may help you to avoid unintended consequences.

Join with these people to discuss your ideas, providing a safe space for them to brainstorm around your solutions. Once you have the input, take responsibility for your vision and passion. Now that you are armed with information that can guide you toward success, make the decision to do something every day toward that passion.

Reconnecting With Common Sense

Common sense is no longer common.

Have you heard people make this statement?

We have so many demanding issues that can be solved using commonsense solutions, and yet we often complicate things so much that nothing seems to get done.

The Empire State Building in New York City took only one year and forty-five days to build, and it took more than seven million work hours. When Kennedy said we would go into space, it took under a decade to deliver that vision. In contrast to these accomplishments, I heard recently that a restroom in Central Park cost two million dollars and over a year for construction!

How is it possible for it to have taken that long or cost that much money to build a park public bathroom? It shows how much we have lost in common sense. This same lack of common sense is what has led to the world of illnesses and diseases that now consumes our country's resources, productivity, time, and energy.

What is the cost? Can we calculate the cost of creating an unhealthy society?

If we were to count the cost in hard numbers, it would be so astronomical that it would be clear that all reason has left the building.

Consider the cost to business of having productivity consumed by factors like these:

- Lack of energy and focus caused by employees in poor health
- Stress that causes presenteeism (working while sick, stressed, and unfocused)
- Chronic illnesses that cause absenteeism
- Sedentary employees that sit at a desk all day and become prone to obesity, repetitive motion injuries, workers' compensation injuries, and more
- Inefficiency and slow progress because of time lost due to health issues

If business managers evaluated all the ancillary costs involved with employee illness and stress, they would see that designing a healthy working environment could save money and time and provide other advantages as well.

A healthy corporate environment:

- Nurtures the natural way people work
- Allows for movement
- Promotes good nutrition

- Supports family and community
- Offers a corporate culture that inspires and supports everyone

Fostering this kind of healthy work environment is only one idea that demonstrates a return to commonsense reasoning, a return to critical thinking, and a return to solution-driven decision making.

What is ironic is that as we think this way and act based upon these simple philosophies, our problems will actually become smaller. They will become chunked down into segments that are more easily handled.

When we seek natural and commonsense solutions to problems, we begin to develop a society that is healthier, more productive, joyful, and easier to navigate. We can develop systems with fewer problems and use mechanisms that enable us to act upon these problems in ways that bring faster resolution. As a result, healthy outcomes will occur more and more.

So, when a problem arises, turn toward solutions that demonstrate common sense. For instance, if you or a loved one were diagnosed with a health problem, you wouldn't only ask: *Why me?* or *Why my loved one?*

Instead, you would analyze the problem using commonsense tactics.

Here are four questions to ask yourself:
1. *What happened?*
2. *Why did it happen?*
3. *What was the root cause?*
4. *How can we create a solution that will reverse the symptoms and eliminate the root cause?*

This can be applied to any symptom of life that comes up. A broken pipe? Perhaps it broke when the weather got cold. The root cause? Perhaps the pipe needed to be weatherized and wasn't. A solution that will reverse the problem and eliminate the root cause? The pipe can be repaired and weatherized so it won't crack again when the weather gets cold.

If you don't ask the right questions, you will soon have to replace a broken pipe again. This is common sense in action!

There are unlimited options for societal discourse, health, and living a passionate and joyful life. The first step is in the questions you ask. The next step is in the answers that come from that. With those answers, you can gather your resources, tools, equipment, people, loved ones, and support system to help further break down those options. The last phase is to act and reassess, act and reassess, and act and reassess again, staying flexible and able to move with nature as you assess all the options that are right for you.

CHAPTER TWO

The Current State of Healthcare and Medicine

WESTERN MEDICINE

Western medicine has been receiving its share of bad press these days. We read about bought-and-paid-for scientific studies that move forward pharmaceutical agendas. We hear about insurance companies that have made it nearly impossible for doctors to do their jobs. The average doctor visit has been shortened to just under eight minutes of actual doctor-patient interaction.

How can Western medicine keep up otherwise with the demand?

There are endless lines of sick people seeking help. Western medicine has proven to be a failure at keeping our society healthy. However, the innovation that has come from Western medicine is astonishing.

The rate at which technological advances are being made is astounding. From artificial organs and limbs to the regrowth of organs from stem cells, these innovations are moving us more toward a marriage between science and humanity in which we are destined to be part machine and part human. In addition, technological innovations have advanced diagnostics and emergency medicine significantly.

While we recognize the value of these innovations, we need to address the failures of Western medicine. It is time to rediscover the Hippocratic Oath that has as a primary tenet the belief that we must *do no harm*.

In the pursuit for better treatments, we have—as a society and as an industry—forgotten this valuable tenet. Now is the time to rediscover why we practice medicine.

Treatment Versus Results

Medicine in the civilized world has been marked by one primary set of discussions. These conversations have been centered on how to treat the symptoms of illness and disease.

For instance, a patient comes to a doctor with a headache and maybe a little nausea. In the seven-to-ten-minute session, the doctor learns a few short stories of previous health, and having this grand picture laid out, prescribes one drug for the nausea, one for the headache, and eventually, maybe even a third drug to help with further problems or the side effects of the drugs. In this scenario, there is no attempt at constructing a plan to reverse the causes of these symptoms, only to alleviate the symptoms as they are.

What is the result?

In some cases, the patient might be lucky. The drugs may mask the symptoms long enough for the causative factor to leave, or more likely simply be suppressed until it is no longer bioactive. In most instances, however, the symptoms are only suppressed long enough until it is time to take that next dose of the drugs. With the root cause of the illness ignored, the patient will likely find the symptoms recurring and continue to seek relief.

It is unfortunate that with all the money we spend on medicine, both in execution and in research and development, we have somehow forgotten to go after the root causes of disease, illness, or pain.

We have developed a system that is not based on results but is based solely on treatments. A physician is not rewarded for making you better, only for the number of procedures performed. When we pay for procedures rather than results, there is so much room for fraud and abuse. The more specialized and intricate the procedure, the more money paid.

As a result:

- You will meet people who have had not one, but multiple heart stents put in.
- Some people are walking around after multiple knee surgeries or multiple back surgeries.
- We often hear people talking about taking medications for their entire lives.
- People do not get better in the long term from taking these medications, and the number of drugs they are taking often increases every year.
- We still are not achieving healthy outcomes.

I believe that this can change. It only requires a shift in perspective.

Are we open to shifting our perspective?

Reactive Versus Proactive

We have designed our entire system of medicine on being reactive rather than proactive.

For instance, if you are in a car accident, you'll go the emergency room, right?

This is a logical sequence of events following an incident where injury or pain result.

Emergency medicine is strictly reactive in nature. It might seem like it must be that way. To some, there is no way to be proactive in the situation above.

After all, it was an accident, and you can't do anything about accidents, right?

Asking interesting questions as a way to find the bottom line of symptoms has taught me a thing or two. Consider that car accident.

How could you have been proactive in this situation?

Here are some questions I might ask you:

- Did you drink enough water and have enough nutrition to keep you alert while driving?

- Did you put your cell phone away before you started driving?

- Sitting in cars will make you stiff after a while. Did you stretch before getting into the vehicle so your body was relaxed?

- Did you remember to check all your lights and mirrors to make sure you had optimal vision?

These are all proactive activities. Now, they might not have prevented the accident from occurring — although one of them may have. Even so, what these proactive efforts might have done is prepare your body and mind a little more for the activity you were about to do so that you could be at optimal physical and mental health. Being better prepared allows you to handle incidents more readily, to absorb shock more effectively, or to move quickly out of the way of danger.

Being proactive enables us to be prepared for the unexpected. This is why athletes need to train their bodies to be able to handle the physical activity they engage in, as well as learning specific plays and maneuvers.

What does being proactive mean when it comes to medicine on the scale of holistic health?

It means searching for the root causes of disease and illness and working to eliminate those factors.

In ancient Rome, as we discussed in the last chapter, people were getting sick, in part, from the garbage and human waste that was accumulating near the places they lived and gathered. Rather than exclusively reacting to the illnesses, the Romans were also proactive in finding the root causes of the spread of illness. They decided to create a sewer and aqueduct system that moved waste away from densely populated areas.

This infrastructure was created in response to a mindset that sought solutions rather than treatments. This mindset addresses the root causes of obstacles and provides for systemic solutions that aid the multitude as opposed to seeking individual treatments that only affect one person at a time.

Symptoms Versus Root Causes

Seeking treatments for disease symptoms will always be easier because they only focus on what is right in front of them. However, this way will always yield poorer results in the long term than going after systemic solutions to root causes. People are individuals, and they react differently to similar stimuli. What affects one person in one way will affect another person in a different way. Some people have allergic reactions and others do not; the tolerances we have are different. As long as we are dealing exclusively with symptoms, we will be losing the battle toward healthy outcomes.

Going after the root, however, can be daunting. Sometimes the cause is hidden, and it takes some investigation to find out what is really going on before we can develop a solution that will work.

Being proactive requires that we be both attentive and perceptive to realize when something is working less than optimally. It often takes commitment and persistence to develop and implement solutions. In some cases, going after the causative factors might ruffle feathers, and sometimes it takes an entire movement to get the job done. It takes faith, technology, and most importantly, the willingness of industry to change and be flexible. It may take guts to go in a direction that is less popular, or in some cases, costs the industry money, time, or resources.

It is not an easy path to optimum results, but as we've discussed, it is usually pretty simple. It's like eating an apple off a tree instead of ordering a burger out of a window. It's simple, but not always easy.

Western medicine has its place in the annals of health care, but it has failed us in maintaining healthy lives. The time has come for the current system to move aside for a new and more thoughtful approach. The willingness of those who know better ways to stand up and create the change we all desire will determine how long we continue the current state of sick care.

This system is already doomed to failure. It costs too much money and too many lives.

SINGLE-LAYER THINKING

Single-layer thinking is the antithesis of the integrative thought that is required to seek root causes and implement the solutions we've been talking about. Single-layer thinking eliminates all cofactors and refuses to accept alternative ideas.

In the medical arena, this kind of thinking is demonstrated by directives that cannot be altered. Check out the people who are in your industry. See how open they are to alternative ideas around a given challenge. We have all met people who are single-layer thinkers, but this kind of philosophy can also be evident in industries, in widespread standards of practice and protocols. In the medical field, it is easily seen in the protocols that are prescribed.

Follow this scenario:

> *Patient XYZ enters a hospital. He is displaying signs and symptoms of whooping cough.*
>
> *Without undergoing any tests, the patient leaves the hospital with a set of drugs and protocols for bronchitis.*

> The patient returns to the hospital later in the day due to an allergic reaction to one of the drugs.
>
> Patient, suspecting whooping cough after reviewing his symptoms, asks for a test for this disease. The staff is resistant. The patient must explain to the hospital it is a test that the lab can do readily and easily.
>
> It turns out the hospital has not tested for whooping cough in over a decade. The patient is told whooping cough has the same protocol as bronchitis, so they don't do that test.

This is an example of single-layer thinking. In my estimation, single-layer thinking is the inability to see beyond what is directly in front of us. Single-layer thinkers are not able to recognize the cause and effect that they have on the world. So, they isolate their thinking to rote protocols rather than challenge themselves to think outside the box. They refuse to see what *could* be different.

High Blood Sugar Means Diabetes

A single-layer thinker will automatically respond to a given stimulus with a programmed response. For example, if someone who is exhibiting high blood sugar went to a physician who is a single-layer thinker, the physician may only see the symptom *high blood sugar* and immediately call it diabetes.

Before we know it, the patient will be on a protocol to manage that diabetes and will be told that they will need to stay on it for the rest of their life. That patient will receive a sentence with no chance of parole. They will be chained to this label from now on.

Let's contrast that scenario with a visit to a physician who is a complex thinker and who follows a critical mindset.

Noting the high blood sugar, the first thing they might do is ask a variety of questions:

- What did you eat today?
- What is your diet usually like?
- Do you have any family history of diabetes?
- Has your diet changed in the last year?
- How have you been feeling?
- Has your lifestyle or anything else changed recently?

This physician will continue to ask leading questions that guide toward a set of possible causative factors. Once all the data is compiled, a decision will be made about the treatment protocol. Ideally, the protocol will address the root cause of the problem, not just the symptoms. In addition, it will be designed to be a good fit for the patient's lifestyle.

If You're Fat, You Must Be Eating Too Many Calories

Calories in and calories out: it's that simple! Right?

If you are overweight, you have probably heard this kind of proclamation. It amazes me how often I still hear people in the medical and fitness world say things like this.

Many proclaim that a fat person must be eating too many calories, although it's become pretty clear that this is not exactly the case. Factors involved in the equation are numerous, but the single-layer thinker will stick with that one idea.

In contrast, the multi-layer thinker, when meeting an overweight patient, will begin with a list of questions that go beyond such a simple equation.

They may ask questions like these:

- What are you eating, and how much?
- How are you feeling?
- How balanced are your hormone levels?
- How efficiently are you processing nutrients?
- What nutrients are you deficient in?
- Is there anything you may be allergic to that is interfering in your body's digestive process?

- How are you processing the nutrients you are consuming?
- What environmental factors are impacting you at home and work?
- What kind of toxin load are you carrying?

Questions like these are designed to help begin the diagnostic process so that root causes are found and results are achieved. The current approach to our overweight population is lacking in many ways, and it has hurt many people.

Have you gone through diet after diet and had each one fail to work?

How many workout routines have you tried in an effort to become healthy?

How many overweight people have been asked questions besides how much they were eating? How many have had a physician work toward solving the root causes of their weight issues?

Our outcomes would be so much better if we changed our standards of practice so we treat weight problems by looking for root causes. The kind of in-depth questioning we're talking about works great in the fitness world as well. When we begin to bridge the gaps between the medical industries, the fitness industry, and the holistic health industry, our outcomes will become better and the health of our communities will return. Think of how much time can be saved with a society of healthy people being productive happy members of their community.

Evaluation Based on Visual Perception

In the world of fitness and kinesthetic health, the visual evaluation is standard practice in the industry. Professionals will put clients through a series of movements and visually assess imbalance and weakness. They may even use visual tools to assess range of motion and the extent of movement where pain begins.

Unfortunately, visual assessments are subjective. If we go to four practitioners, we will hear four different perceptions of what is going on. Additionally, visual assessments only tell a piece of the puzzle. We might see something that is not there, or not see something that is. For example, a hip may be internally rotated and, therefore, we make a judgment or diagnosis based on seeing that. What we did not see was that the ankle had an injury five months prior, and the hip was compensating for an imbalance in the ankle. In order to gain that knowledge, we must be willing to ask questions and do more than just a visual assessment.

Palpation is a great physical assessment that will provide more information about what is happening in the client's body than a visual assessment. From palpation, we can ascertain temperature differentiation, swelling, loss of circulation, ligament tenderness, areas of edema, and trigger points of pain—both physical and in some cases, emotional as well. Practitioners who have honed these skills sense apprehension in tissue by touch. They are able to discriminate tension from stress, rather than from injury or scar tissue, and more.

As medical professionals build assessment muscles, their thinking shifts from single-layer thinking to multi-layer, multi-planar thinking. As we incorporate more and more knowledge from other disciplines into our own, always tweaking what we do, we will achieve better and better outcomes. We will learn to leave techniques behind when they provide less than optimum results and turn to new information and new skill development.

A whole world of possibility awaits the brave who venture forth into the unknown and bring back the new.

INSULAR PRACTICE

One of the causes of the modern case of Western medicine we find ourselves experiencing is that of the insular practice. We could describe them as *doctors on islands*.

I was recently speaking to a group of doctors who are on the edge of new science, new protocols, and new treatments. The overwhelming sentiment was that each felt that they were out in the frontier lands, practicing and innovating these new techniques, and they had no one to talk with about what they were doing.

These doctors are on the cutting edge, and they have no real forum to discuss what is working for them in the field for fear of the consequences of working outside the industry standards of practice. When someone decides to be innovative and achieves good results, they should be heralded and praised by the community. They should be able to discuss what they are doing with others in the field. This is how medicine truly grows. When those who are in the field can express what is and isn't working for them, they can inform and receive feedback from others in the field and create treatments based on that feedback.

Fearing the insurance companies and American Medical Association (AMA) retribution, doctors who are doing this cutting-edge medicine often do it in hiding, and the only praise or feedback they receive is from themselves. Medical tourism has been popping up all over the world because so many of these frontier doctors are taking their medicine to countries that are more flexible in their approach to health for their communities.

The biggest fear regarding insular practices is that the innovators will completely pass our system by. The wealthy will be able to take advantage of the advances in medicine, but the system won't be able to move fast enough to keep up. If the system can't keep up, then the outcomes will be limited, and pain and suffering will continue, especially among the poor.

One-Sided Education

Where do we start?

We have created such an overwhelming conundrum for ourselves, it sometimes feels like all is lost.

The solution to any set of obstacles or challenges is typically simple, yet it can be difficult. Mostly, we don't know what we don't know. Therefore, we need others to join with their talents and gifts.

We require education, but our educational system is inadequate these days. We have given up critical thinking and deductive reasoning and replaced them with test-taking skills. Instead of inspiring curiosity, we ask for memorization of mundane material. We punish kids for being outspoken or precocious rather than praising them and nurturing those aspects of them. We need to go back to a well-rounded education that includes life skills, cognitive thinking, and deductive reasoning.

As long as our educational system is determined to remain the same, our medical schools will consist of students who can only listen and regurgitate information rather than think critically and diagnose thoughtfully. We will continue to turn out doctors who are trained to meet with their patients for seven minutes, listen to symptoms, and regurgitate the drug information that goes with the symptoms. Rinse and repeat!

Closed-Minded to Other Possibilities

These industry-wide symptoms occur because our new doctors are subjected to this style of education. I think the most dangerous of these symptoms is that the industry is fairly closed-minded to other possibilities and techniques.

I recently saw this popular internet saying: *People eat junk food without batting an eye, but offer them something healthy and they become researchers.*

It is difficult to bring about changes in the education system because there is a push in the industry to keep the status quo. By closing students' minds to possibility, they are chained to their limitations.

What if a method wasn't working well, but someone down the street had a better way?

How would you communicate that information to the closed-minded practitioner?

I remember when I was young and my grandmother was dying of pancreatic cancer. I had been studying herbology, nutrition, and health. I advised her to try taking shark cartilage, which might help with the cancer. One day, a couple of months into taking the shark cartilage, she went back for tests and they showed that her counts were all moving in the right direction. She was getting better and feeling better.

Her doctor asked her what she was doing differently. He couldn't believe how fast she was improving. So, she excitedly told him that she was taking shark cartilage and shared some research about how it was helping people with cancer. The doctor immediately changed his disposition and told her emphatically that what she was taking was not what was helping her and that it was all bunk. It was a long time ago, and I am paraphrasing here; however, you get the gist of the conversation.

My grandmother had the wind taken right out of her sails. The joy she was feeling was replaced with hopelessness; the new health she was feeling was replaced with weakness. The shark cartilage remained untouched and she passed two months later.

In an industry about health, it can be a death sentence to be closed-minded to the possibilities. Remember, we are *practicing* medicine; there is always so much to learn from all modalities and cultures. I truly believe that I lost my grandmother prematurely because of the response from the one person's hands she chose to put her life in. I wonder: what lesson did he learn?

Integration

I have said that solutions to obstacles are simple. So, what is the solution to closed-mindedness? It is education in a variety of other fields within the industry.

Wouldn't it be cool if every medical school required students to learn about the way medicine is practiced in other cultures?

I can envision them taking a class from a Native American medicine man and a Chinese acupuncturist. I can see them learning herbology, homeopathy, healing touch, and more.

Inside modern medicine, we can already find evidence of the medicine from ancient cultures. It is a shame that most doctors don't know the herbal roots of modern drugs. There has been such an emphasis on pharmacology and chemistry that they often forget the origin of our medicines; many of the active ingredients we use are derived from herbs.

Integration with the natural way of life is always more effective. The evidence is all around us. In medicine, we are beginning to see medical offices integrating so they can present patients with multiple modalities and specializations. The greatest benefit of integration and open-minded education is that it translates to *all* parts of our lives. When we integrate thoughts with others, we can begin to collaborate and cooperate more and our results will increase in quality and in speed.

When you are unable to bring a plan to reality, you may find that a lack of integration has blocked your progress. Think about how integration could have impacted your plan.

What if you had a team of people dedicated to what you wanted to create?

What if these people were chock-full of the expertise you needed to accomplish that passion of yours?

How many people could benefit from that kind of integration of skills and talents?

If our medical system could be flexible and move swiftly, so many lives could be saved. And what if we extended this integration between industries? It would have an impact that would radiate outward throughout the community.

Here are some examples:

- Doctors could talk to engineers about creating more sanitary sewage systems, water filtration, and delivery structures.

- While designing infrastructure, engineers could be talking to the city planners and architects about how to create towns so they thrive financially and foster the betterment of health.

- Together, professionals could figure out how local food would best be cultivated, walkways be made safe and readily available, homes be built with no chemicals and shielded from electrical waves that cause illness.

- Industries could work together so that everyone benefits, with jobs created and lives renewed.

This blissful integration of thought, along with the openness to be flexible and put into action what we learn, is beneficial now rather than later.

CHAPTER THREE

Why I Do What I Do

MY PAIN

> *The journey to enlightenment is shrouded in the darkest of shadows.*

There is a wonderful and painful mystery in the universe, and that is the mystery of duality. Duality, the way I use it, is the clashing of two opposing experiences. Light and dark, positive and negative, high and low, near and far—you get the picture. To understand the light and truly appreciate it, many times we must forge through the darkness and muck.

This duality has been intertwined in me throughout my entire life. As a very young child, I was molested and sexually abused multiple times. I was three when this happened for the first time and completely unaware of the impact that it would have on my entire life. Being physically sexualized before my brain could understand the intricacies of a mature sexual nature shaped most of my teenage and young adult experiences. Innocence lost at such a young age has also shaped, to some extent, my inquisitive nature because I was constantly asking *why*.

I never experienced childhood in the way a child protected and innocent might have, but my darkness has allowed me to be of service to others in a way I never imagined. I have had the privilege to work with women who have been abused. I have had the privilege of helping them heal the pain and shame stuck in their bodies. My darkness has allowed others to experience light.

Pain has been my best friend and worst enemy. It is truly a subjective experience to be in pain. For some, pain debilitates and for others, it motivates; for some, it is a barrier and for others, it is a challenge to be overcome. To be completely honest, for most of my personal life it has been a barrier for me, an almost insurmountable obstacle that kept me imprisoned in the circumstances I was in. However, on the opposite side of the spectrum, for most of my career it has been the biggest blessing. It has been a growth opportunity for me as a man, as a healer, and as a human being.

Without the pain I carry, this growth would not have been possible. I have grown up and mastered the work I do because of the experiences of pain and illness that have shaped my life. Seeking enlightenment through the darkness and traveling the journey of a warrior healer has filled me with the blessings from all the lives I have been able to touch.

Hormone and Chemistry Imbalance

What we don't know *can* hurt us.

That is indeed the case with hormonal and chemical imbalances in the body. Hormones regulate more than our sex drive. They regulate everything from how efficiently our organs work to our mood, our recovery from injury, muscle growth, how we store fat, and how we process incoming nutrition. Hormones play a vital role in every function of our physiology.

Forty years ago, there was so much to be learned about this subject. We have truly come a long way in our understanding of the functioning of the body. We have learned a great deal about how different systems interact within us and are just beginning to learn the extent to which our internal chemistry interacts with the external world.

There are studies now that show how lights while we are sleeping affect the pineal gland and have a detrimental physical outcome in sleep patterns. We know that the chemistry of our environment is in direct opposition to having a healthy body. Chemicals in pesticides and plastics have made their way into our water supply, added purposefully as well as via runoff and ground contamination, and may cause hormone disruption, which changes the natural functioning of the body.

Have you noticed young girls beginning to go through puberty at six and seven years old? Have you noticed young men prematurely losing their hair and experiencing painful acne issues?

As a growing boy, I was an athlete. I did gymnastics, martial arts, long-distance cycling, played baseball and tennis, and was adept at all these sports. Around age seven, however, I started to experience health issues. I would get migraines and hot flashes. I felt chronically tired and began to cramp a lot. I experienced a great deal of physical pain, as well as emotional ups and downs. By the time I was twelve, I had not begun going through puberty, so I felt like something was drastically wrong. I was gaining weight despite all the physical activity I did, and I was depressed, angry, and not having much fun.

I went to the doctor, and it turned out that I was not producing enough testosterone. To make matters even more complicated, I was producing too much estrogen and my other hormones, such as cortisol,

HGH, DHEA, and prolactin were acting in opposition to each other. Basically, my internal chemistry was on the fritz. Not knowing exactly what to do back then, they drugged me into puberty with shots of replacement testosterone, which began the process of moving me toward puberty. However, not much was known about this treatment, and there were unintended consequences, one of them being the growth of male breast tissue for which I needed reduction surgery at age fourteen.

A brain tumor in my pituitary gland was not found until I was twenty-four. From seven until twenty-four years of age, I was treated and mistreated, diagnosed and misdiagnosed, drugged and mis-drugged. I went to holistic doctors, traditional doctors, naturopaths, acupuncturists, chiropractors, a sports therapist, endocrinologists, and more, trying to find answers to the pain I live with daily. At forty-two years old, with modern diagnostics, combined with genetic testing, we are closer to finding the root.

Physical Injuries

Having been an athlete with severe hormonal imbalances and not knowing how or what to do to deal with these things, I simply kept going as a young man would. Playing through the pain and never stretching enough, I caused myself injury after injury.

As I often tell people now, I have great stories for the grandkids about all the things I did with this body. I had injuries from gymnastics, baseball, martial arts, and tennis. They caused problems in my lower back, shoulders, knees, and more.

I suffered sudden and sharp painful cramps and didn't find out the reason until years later. Because of the lower testosterone levels, my muscles could not heal fast enough from activity and would hold on to lactic acid. Recovery time was slow after physical activity, whether it was for practice or for fun. Pain was always just around the corner.

I grew up in a time before cell phones and a thousand television channels. There was no point to staying in the house; we were brought up to dismiss pain and keep going. For me, my pain was intriguing enough to me that I chose to study how to help people relieve pain as a search for my own health.

My Search for a Cure

By eighteen years old, fresh out of high school, I had already learned about aromatherapy and herbology, and I self-medicated with any natural herbal drug I could find that would help me out of my head and out of my pain. I ended up going to a naturopathic physician who prescribed me a homeopathic remedy.

That remedy, combined with environmental factors including sun and heat stroke, provided a perfect storm and sent my body into anaphylactic shock.

I ended up at a hospital emergency room being resuscitated for over twenty-six minutes. For days afterward, they tested my respirations and were confounded that none of the equipment was picking up any carbon in my outbreath.

Finally, still in the hospital, I woke up one morning and said, "I need to go to school and become a healer."

There was no tunnel with light at the end of it, but I did get a direction that was steady and clear. My search for a cure had begun.

Massage was the first stop on that journey in my professional life. In massage school, I quickly earned respect from the owner and head trainer. After the third month, I ran her clinic and began the first corporate wellness training at her school. We happened to have Intel, Techtronic, and Nike offices close to the school, and I wanted to reach out to those companies for more clients.

After a health fair, where I worked on Richard Simmons and Victoria Jackson, I worked on a couple of professional sports players who had a game that evening. The players liked my work so much that I ended up on the court that night. Eventually, an internship began my career as *The Performance Therapist*.

Since then, I have never ceased to educate myself. As I interned with the professional team, I also trained under a multitude of other modalities. I wanted to learn as much as I could from as many perspectives as I could, mainly because I wanted them to work on me. I studied mindset, nutrition, and chemistry. I studied scientific arts like kinesiology, physical therapy, chiropractic, massage, and eventually, functional medicine and lifestyle design. I studied the energetic arts such as Reiki, tantra, and shamanism. The more I studied, the more questions I asked. The more questions I found answers for, the more questions popped up.

I started out trying to solve my own problems, and the more I learned, the more I found that I could help others. In this pursuit for a cure for my pain and illnesses, I have now helped thousands of people achieve a level of freedom from their pain and illness.

The biggest lesson in all of this?

I learned that I needed help.

No matter what I believed I knew, there were, and still are, elements that are hidden from my sight.

Mentorship, doctor, healer, coach — it doesn't matter, as long as we have someone other than ourselves to shed light where we cannot see.

The healthiest and happiest communities in the world are the ones that are centered in being support systems for each other. In the meantime, as technology improves and diagnostics and treatments become better known, my journey to healing will continue, and my path as a healer will deepen, strengthen, and mature.

I started out by saying the pain is subjective. A ten on the pain scale for me could be a five for someone else. We already know that a woman's pain tolerance during childbirth is more than a man could ever handle — kudos for the wife and all the moms out there!

My pain has caused my life's greatest pleasures. To be a part of and a witness to the healing and relief of so many people over the years has been such a blessing. I have witnessed the rawest of emotions being expressed and released, the deepest of pains being let go, as well as the potential of elite athletes being realized. What a gift this pain has given — to me and to others as well.

I must say that this chapter took the longest of any other chapter in the book. At times, I became caught up in the drama of circumstances, forgetting that gratitude for the experiences is exactly what allowed me to face the toughest emotions for me: *forgiveness* and *self-love*.

This is an area that I am in direct conversation with regularly. I love the philosophy of Ho'oponopono: *I am sorry, please forgive me, I love you, thank you.*

The pain that we place in our own minds can be the most intense of all — the pain in the memories we choose to store and the patterns and habits we choose to continue. The most destructive words are the words we speak to ourselves in the deepest crevices of our subconscious.

The most intense of all pain is the emotional pain we cause our own selves. Being diligent to quiet those voices has been my greatest challenge, and it delivers the greatest rewards. I know that the greatest gift I could leave to my family is the healing of my own self-talk. It is a work in process for sure.

MY PROCESS

I want to talk about my process here, the way I come up with solutions to my own situations. I want to share with you how I organize my thoughts and keep myself in my lanes so that I can communicate well with those whom I am teaching and training, so they can have a clear idea of what it is that I do and why.

How does your mind work?

Your process may be different, but reading about mine may help you to examine the way you organize your thoughts and help you improve your approach to problem solving.

My process sometimes takes a while. I am an auditory kinesthetic, which means I have a committee in my mind, so the process can take time. It may be the same for you, so be patient.

One final thought before we move on: It is helpful to have other people—friends and family—who will give you honest and positive feedback. Not only can they help you speed up the process, but they can also lessen that pain that comes from doing it alone.

How My Mind Thinks About Something

I tend to find interrelationships between all things. I find the ways in which things are connected, the way things combine, the way things attach. It is like string theory and quantum physics, the notion that every action has a connection to countless consequences that then have a string that goes out to experience in the world. I try to find the strings that create the best outcomes at the beginning before I start. You can liken this to the way some people play chess — playing ten moves ahead in their minds, as opposed to just playing the next move or two.

It also reminds me of the Chinese, who make hundred-year plans and five-hundred-year plans instead of ten-year plans for building a city.

That is how my process works. I think about how the things interrelate, inter-correlate, and then I find a solution that gives the most expedient result that can be accomplished.

Here is an example. I was watching a show called *Impact Theory* and a guest spoke about fat loss. He broke down the chemical makeup of fat, which is a long chain of carbon, hydrogen, and oxygen. He said that most people think we lose the fat from our bodies through sweat, urine, and stool, but only 20 percent is lost through those means, while 80 percent is actually lost through our breath.

So, listening to that program, here is how my mind worked:

After hearing this guest give this statistic, my mind went to *breath work*. Next, it recalled that *breath work works on the lymphatic and the fat system in order to release fat.*

I thought about these facts: *We are breathing and 80 percent of fat is released through our breath.* My mind tied those two together. *If you are doing breath work, you are going to lose fat — and you are going to lose weight.*

Next, my brain tied these ideas into others related to it: *emotional release and rebirthing,* and all the different ways in which *we use breath to release emotion.*

I knew that *fat is made up of stored energy* and *stored memories and stored emotions are forms of stored energy.* Now, my mind connected breath work and emotional release with fat loss.

Do you see how we can interrelate, inter-correlate, and combine all these ideas? *Breath work, the science of fat loss, and emotional release* are connected. That is how my brain thinks.

The Steps That I Go Through to Shift or Change

Your beliefs determine the way you process your experiences, the way you operate and react to your environment, and the world around you. To heal, it is sometimes necessary to change a belief system, and this can be difficult.

I go through an internal, followed by an external, process for shifting or changing my belief systems. First, and I teach this to my patients and my students, is to recognize that when this shift or change happens, you will be leaving something behind. You must figure out what you are leaving behind and come to grips with it. You must accept the loss, grieve, and release it. In effect, you are leaving behind who you have been up to that point so that you can be who you really want to be.

When we shift and change, it is painful; transformation is a painful experience. Think about the lobster in the shell. It is not until the shell grows too tight around its body that it sheds it and grows another. Shifts and changes can be painful. There needs to be a grieving process over shifting and changing.

The second thing I do, after coming to terms with the idea that I do not know who I am going to be tomorrow, is to start breathing.

Then I tell myself: *If I am to be who I want to be, then I get to create that.*

After you grieve, you have an opening to create something new.

Sometimes a person might be trying to change their belief system to believe they can achieve more than they previously thought they could. When it comes to going from a silver medal mentality to a gold medal or world championship mentality, it might be hard to envision what you are leaving behind. In these cases, you should grieve the pain of never having had that experience yet, in order to open up the space to believe that you can.

Then, you must attempt to internally feel the experience before it happens. There is a concept in hypnotherapy that if you image yourself doing an activity, your muscles will fire in the exact same way they would if you were actually doing it. This is what you are attempting to do.

Meditation, visualization, and physically journaling — writing down how I want that change to look in the future — are the last parts of my process. And then I sit in faith and believe that it already is so. This is not easy. It is a lifelong, ongoing process, and there is always more to do.

Dealing With Outside Perspectives

This is a big one because most of my life I have been deeply affected by others' opinions and perspectives about me. I have learned that I have huge amounts of blame and shame — a victim mentality — around outside perspectives. When I deal with outside perspectives, I've found that it helps if I try to go back from *heart* to *head,* which is unusual for me. I try to use logic to explain to myself why it is that the way I am looking at something is, at least in my view, more efficient, more effective, or gets better results.

I search for the scientific reasoning behind my perspective, so that I can explain it in a logical way. Then, I go back to the heart of the matter and look at what causes somebody to believe what they believe, so that I can empathize with the position that they have, rather than categorizing them as *wrong* for a perspective that may not be as efficient.

When I deal with outside perspectives, I try not to use words like *wrong* or *bad;* instead, I think about it in terms of one idea not being quite as effective or efficient in getting results as another.

In one of my classes, I had a student who had been a professor for many years. I was a little bit afraid of teaching her. She had some different perspectives. Rather than reacting in the middle of the class, I sat back with it, and then I asked her a few questions to uncover why she was thinking the way she was thinking.

Then, I gave her my perspective and she shifted where she was coming from based on this new information. First, I took the emotion from my reaction to not being understood, and then, I came back into my heart so I could be inquisitive about why she was thinking that way. It's about honoring the other person's perspective as well as your own.

MY RESULTS

I know that some of you are just holding on, grasping your last straw, your last string, the last nerve. You may have been in pain your whole life and do not know anything else. You may have been searching and seeking an answer to something that nobody has been able to help you with. I share my results here because I believe that they will give a perspective of possibility and hope for those people who believe there is none left.

My results come from the process I use to shift and change, the way that my mind thinks about things, and the steps I go through myself. These are also the steps I use with my patients, with the people whom I have worked with to help transform their lives.

I want to stress that results require several steps: taking a holistic view of a situation, seeing all the aspects, the interrelationships, all the correlations, and then moving forward with a strategic plan to change. If you are going to be an athlete, and you want to win a gold medal, you must create a plan. You cannot throw stuff up on a wall, all willy-nilly-like.

It is the same with business planning. You can't just throw together a marketing plan. Successful plans must have processes, and often, need outside help. The results I attained in my story were a direct response to the systems and processes that worked for me. You must take your opportunity to find the systems and processes that will work for you.

I'll give you these two caveats: first, do it with the holistic view in mind, and second, look to the consequences, to the consequences, to the consequences, so that you know what is coming from the actions you are putting forth today.

Gained and Lost Over Five Hundred Pounds

Having already shared about some of my medical and health challenges, I have a perspective to share on weight loss as well. I have attempted almost every mainstream strategy to lose weight. Over the years, I have lost over five hundred pounds in total. I've lost and gained back, lost and gained back—too many times to count.

My highest weight was three hundred and thirty-seven pounds and I am five foot eight. At that point, I looked more like a grape than a person. I have had liposuction. I have tried healthy diets. I have tried fad diets. I have tried vegan diets. I have tried eating organic. I have gone to medical doctors and other medical professionals.

I was told by more than one doctor that I would never lose weight. Ever. That my hormones and chemistry were so out of balance that it was impossible for my body to lose weight. I was basically told that I would gain weight until I died from it—or from a disease that went with it.

That perspective was not a perspective that was okay with me. I had been in the health field my whole life and I know that, as wonderful as doctors may be, as well trained as they may be, they are still, after all, only practicing medicine. The word *practicing*, by default, means that *they don't know everything* and should not be taken 100 percent at their word.

Sometimes you must buck the system. Or replace the "b" in that sentence with an "f" if you like—that's often the way I say it! I have had the experience of bucking the system. The result: Yes, I have been able to lose weight. Yes, I have been able to cut my body size. Even though doctors told me it wouldn't happen, I was able to achieve results.

Those experiences have given me an ability to understand and empathize with people who are struggling. My experiences, my struggles, enabled me to create unique processes for other people, one person at a time. I wanted to share my results because I want to help you have hope and faith. Whatever ailments you have—weight problems, chronic pain, or disease—*there is an answer.*

It is only a matter of asking the right questions and finding the key to your lock. When we find your key, we can open you up and achieve those results you so deserve.

Maintaining a Positive Outlook Even When Results Are Slow

People will tell you that you must stay positive, even when results are slow to come. I won't tell you this. I want to debunk the notion that you must maintain a positive outlook even when you're frustrated. I also want to debunk the notion that you need to sit in your pain when the results are slow.

What do I mean by that?

You must feel.

We are emotional beings and we must feel. Part of being able to maintain a healthy outlook is knowing when your subconscious is spewing negative garbage at you. Being able to feel the pain of that negative garbage your body and your mind is spewing at you is the only way, at least I have found, to transform it.

Unless you are willing to sit in *what is,* you will never be able to experience *what is coming*.

Suppose you are doing amazing, positive, and wonderful things, but the results are slow, you are feeling distress and pain, and you are feeling discouraged. Suppose you try to shove down your feelings. While you force the positive feeling out, that subconscious negative pain is going to take over your behavior, and results will come even slower.

Part of maintaining a positive outlook is expressing your feelings in the moments when you are feeling negative, then following it by being grateful.

You might be saying to yourself: *Why in the world would I be grateful for negative feelings?*

Negative feelings are an honest, natural, and necessary part of the process. Negative feelings often show you the places in which you need to grow.

The worst thing in the world is to shove down and hide the way you are feeling. It will take some courage to step out of your comfort zone and feel the pain you are experiencing, but it is the only way to have power over your progress. Keep in mind that benefits are on their way, and then you can maintain a positive outlook even when experiencing negative emotions.

Getting Outside Help

We are conditioned in our society to believe that the hero did it all by himself. The best player in baseball stands at the home plate with the bat in his hands alone, silencing the crowd. The pitcher, who might be the other team's hero in the moment, is standing on their mound alone. This is the American sport, the American dream, standing on your own two feet and being a success. But no one—and this is universally true—no one did it alone.

There is no such thing as a person being an island. You can't wake up born alone on an island, never meet another human being, and become a success in your life, right? Everything that you accomplish comes from your relationships with other people. And getting outside help, mentorship, education, and friendships that are positive will help you grow. Getting outside help is the glue that fastens your results together.

Your support system is your stability; these are the people keeping you together when everything wants to fall apart. Your team is the glue that binds you, that makes you so strong and invincible. When you are going through the worst of it, your team carries you ahead, carries you forward. So, getting outside help is the most important aspect to any transformation, to any growth.

Just as every professional athlete has an entourage, every successful businessperson has a secretary, an assistant, associates—a team that helps grow their business and grow their abilities. Get yourself outside help. Get a team.

CHAPTER FOUR

The Future of Medicine

DO WE ENHANCE THE SYSTEM OR START OVER?

You never change things by fighting the existing reality. To change something, build a new model that makes the existing model obsolete.

This quote is attributed to Buckminster Fuller, who was a famous architect and philosopher. It means that, rather than fighting *what is*, we should create something better, put it next door, and let people choose.

We know the current health system is broken. Should we try to enhance the current system or should we start over from scratch and create something new?

Enhancing the current system would be a mistake, and it would be a very costly mistake. It would take a lot of money and the results would not cover those costs. The smartest thing for us to do is to start over from scratch. First, we need to figure out what the causes of disease and other health problems are. Then, we must put into process the changes and shifts that will create a healthy society from the beginning to the end, from the bottom to the top. That is the smartest and least expensive route to solving the problems of our medical and health system.

What We Are Currently Doing

What we are currently doing in our medical system is finding pathologies and trying to treat them by isolating properties out of plants and turning them into drugs. We are then feeding those drugs to people in enormous amounts. A person older than sixty in this country may swallow eighteen or more pills per day.

These drugs have impacted our water quality; it has been found that, especially in communities where there are older folks, that the water may be riddled with pharmaceutical medications. Whether you are drinking water from the tap or drinking it from plastic bottles, you may be ingesting these pharmaceutical drugs.

So, this is what we are currently doing. We have created this system, thinking that it will improve health, but it is failing. Our efforts are focused on trying to put Band-Aids on symptoms with drugs.

We keep treating; we keep applying Band-Aids, and meanwhile, our health system is out of control. We have some of the worst results of any medical system in the civilized societies of this world. What we are currently doing is not working. It is the wrong philosophy.

We take isolated compounds out of nature to use on disease, but that is not how those chemicals work in nature. We are literally deciding as a people that what we can do is better than what God could do. We take God's creation, bastardize it, and feed it to people, and that is proving to cause more problems than it helps.

As a result, our medical system is causing more ill health than it is helping to alleviate. This generation is the first that is going to live a shorter life span than the previous generation, and that is directly caused by the health-care system that we currently have.

Why Enhancing the System Yields Limited Results

Some suggest that we put our efforts into enhancing the current system, but all that will mean is bigger Band-Aids on wounds that will continue to grow bigger. Enhancing the current system will not address the underlying philosophical reason that the system is broken to begin with.

It is like taking a bad computer operating system and, instead of replacing it with an operating system that is bug-free, going in and searching for bugs. I do not know if you have ever searched for bugs, but you will find them. There will be many. And when you think they are all gone, they are going to come back and in greater numbers.

Why try to enhance a buggy system, a broken system, when you can create a new one that includes the best parts of the old system?

What Does Starting Over Look Like?

To start over, first we must take a step back and look at the bigger picture, keeping our focus on the root causes of the problems.

So, what is the root cause of illness? Why are people sick?

If you look across the board, many people are sick because they do not get *enough*—not enough proper, rich nutrition, not enough movement, not enough sleep. When it comes to many factors that are essential for good health, our bodies do not get enough. Ironically, we have created a food system that feeds us way *too much*—but the food is highly processed and has little nutritional value. So, although we are poorly nourished, we are growing larger and larger.

After we look at the root causes, we need to try to alter them. We need to consider possible solutions. In addition, we also need to figure out how to create a society that can access our solutions.

Suppose we want to eat a diet with less processed food, but higher nutritional value. Besides deciding what this diet should include, we also must look at accessibility. What do we have to do to make this kind of food more accessible?

And we must go down that rabbit hole of asking more questions, finding the solutions, and then starting from a new beginning.

If we want healthy results, we need to think about what that result looks like. We must ask the question: *What does that society look like?*

Then we backtrack and figure out how it happens.

We ask: *What are the causes of those good results?* Then we can create the society to match that philosophy. That is what starting over looks like.

HEALTH IS NOT ABOUT MEDICAL CARE

I think that there is a big misconception about healthcare and medicine. The healthcare system and the medical system are not the same. The truth is that health and medical care are two completely separate things.

What is the difference between health and medicine?

Medical care happens in an emergency.

The emergency could be:

- An injury, like a broken bone or a laceration
- A problem with chemistry so the body isn't able to maintain homeostasis (balance)
- A sickness caused by a virus or a bacterial infection

These are all cases that could be considered an emergency, and in these cases, you would seek medical emergency care.

Health is not about medical care. Health is about how we respond to the environment around us. The manner in which we respond determines how healthy we are. The environment's effect on us is so important, from the lighting that we use to the air we breathe.

Medical care is about emergency conditions, while health is about lifestyles. If we can separate the two, we can begin to have a real conversation about how to create health instead of how to treat ill health or emergencies.

Health is about our communities and our day-to-day lives. When we are building our cities, if we start by remembering that health is about our environment, our communities, and our lifestyle, then we will begin shifting the system. We can begin to create something new by designing our societies around being healthy from the very beginning.

Lifestyle Choices

Health is determined by lifestyle choices.

Here are some examples of what I mean by lifestyle choices:

- You can choose to replace the processed fast food of McDonald's with a different kind of fast food—fresh fruits and vegetables.

- You can make the choice to move your body more and to do more outside activities.

- You can stand and move instead of sitting down and looking at a screen for the majority of the time you are on this planet.

- You can learn about what foods affect your inflammatory issues and your autoimmune system and start cutting those out of your diet.

Lifestyle choices are important, and they are often easily implemented if considered in bite-size chunks. Rather than telling yourself to go run a marathon, tell yourself to walk around the block. Make little lifestyle choices at a time. Start habits and create rituals around them so that your lifestyle becomes easy.

This might mean making healthy meals on a Sunday for the entire week, dividing food into portions that you can take to work with you. That is an example of a ritual that you can use to create a healthy lifestyle choice.

Why Lifestyle Is Not Enough

I want to let you off the hook a little bit and explain to you why lifestyle is not enough. We have all heard of those healthy people—the healthiest guys in the world—who die of a heart attack while jogging. When you look around and you see people who look healthy and fit, many of them may actually have unbalanced hormones or other internal problems, and their bodies are not working the way they should. Lifestyle is not enough.

You can choose to eat healthier and move more but you still need to deal with environmental issues. If your water and your air are being poisoned, and you're being constantly bombarded with radio waves and EMF waves, then you still have to manage this barrage of environmental toxins. So, lifestyle is not enough to clean you out, detoxify your body, and de-stress your system.

You might not know that our bodies were not designed to drive in a car at eighty miles an hour, yet many of us do this every day. Moving this way sets us up for adrenal overload, moves us into fight or flight mode, and causes our stress-response system to go out of whack. This causes hormonal imbalances, which leads to stress-related diseases and ailments. We've already discussed how common stress-related ailments are in America. This is no small issue.

So, lifestyle is important but it is not enough. We need to manage the way we process our environmental health issues as well.

Environment and a Healthy Lifestyle

These environmental issues are extremely important for our health. Regardless of our philosophy on whether we are hurting Mother Earth, regardless of our philosophy about being dominant over the species and over the land as a culture, we are killing ourselves through toxins.

People forget that medicine started with an environmental and societal structure and infrastructure. People forget that our ancestors became sick because their bedroom was on one wall and the other side of the wall was the pig drop, and they had to figure that out. Some were sick because the trash was down on the ground, and rats, flies, or other bugs were transferring germs to people. In each of these cases, the root cause of the spread of illness was in the environment.

When we remember that medicine began as an environmental structure, we can recall how we put in aqueducts to move the water, we put in waste-removal sewage systems to remove the waste from the civilized community so that we would not become sick. When we look at history, we see that the environment is a major part of what creates our health, and that we create this environment.

When we understand this, we will start making shifts in our environment that will play a role in creating a healthier lifestyle. Our society can help move us in a healthy direction. Then, when we make our own individual healthy lifestyle choices, a healthy society will back us up.

INFRASTRUCTURE AND HEALTHCARE

As I was alluding to previously, infrastructure has been used to foster healthcare. People were sick. The people who were watching the people become sick asked why. They realized that they needed to create an infrastructure that reduced toxins in the living space, so they shifted the infrastructure to create a healthier environment, and that reduced illness.

We have shifted backward. We have shifted how we do things, and now we're back to creating illness instead of creating health.

If we remember that building infrastructure is how we improved health in the past, we can see that building our cities into healthy cities is going to be the best money spent. When we take the poisons out, our bodies will automatically begin to heal, and our individual efforts to improve our lifestyles will pay great returns—in health.

Infrastructure is the beginning. When we create our societies, when we look at rebuilding our communities, this is our starting place. We can use new technology as it becomes available. We can figure out how to create societies that are born to be healthy, that create as few stressors as possible, that enhance how we think and how we feel. When we do that, when we create those infrastructures, then we can explode into the possibilities because we are no longer fighting the broken.

When we create a society that is no longer just about *survival,* but is about *health,* we can truly make the society about thriving, inside and out. And we will see a beautiful world develop before us.

The History of Infrastructure as One of the First Responses to Disease

Poor nutrition has been a health problem throughout history. Vitamin and mineral deficiencies caused conditions like scurvy, due to lack of vitamin C. Increasing populations made food shortages common. A lack of high-quality nutrition on a regular basis makes the body weak, and this impacts the functioning of the immune system, making it less effective in dealing with bacteria and viruses.

That is when new agricultural expansions began. People started to develop ways to grow more for large city populations than gathering and hunting did for tribal civilization.

As we began to civilize and combine our tribes into a civilization, we needed to invent ways to move waste and to find water. When environmental issues were well managed through building infrastructure like aqueducts and sewage systems, as we've discussed, the health issues improved.

The Importance of Activists in Our Industry

Activism in our industry is vital. We are the insiders. We know what the causes of diseases are. We know about the toxic overload. Just like in a war, we see the fallout due to the current system. We see what it is doing to our society. We see the disease grow.

We see type I diabetes growing. We see obesity increasing. We see the results of the industry as it is. And being insiders, we have an obligation to be activists and to change the way in which our society creates itself so that we create a healthier society. It is incumbent upon us—*it is our duty.*

It is our duty, as people in the health industry and citizens of the world, to make other people aware of what the industry is doing and what the results are, so that we can actually make lasting change.

Activists are tremendously important, and the more there are, the more effective they can be. When we are working one at a time, it is easy for the opposition to target us. We have had so many in our industry who have been killed, murdered—over seventy-three, I believe—people who were activists who were exposing the failings of the industry. That can happen when there are only a few of us.[2]

But what if we *all* took it upon ourselves to be activists?

They would not be able to shut us down; the message would have to come across. This is why it is important for you — as a physician, as a therapist, as a trainer — to become involved. If you are in the health and fitness industry or the medical industry, you can spread the knowledge you have as an insider and create the legislative changes required to make a healthier community and society.

What You Can Do

What can you do?

First, notice what is happening and ask yourself:

- *What is the cause of this situation?*
- *Do I have a solution?*
- *Whom do I need on my team to help me get this solution actualized?*

If you are an engineer, a city planner, an architect, or a doctor, you can get involved in your local, city, or state governments. You can find out how water is

---

[2] healthnutnews.com/recap-on-my-unintended-series-the-holistic-doctor-deaths

being delivered to homes in your community. You can participate in decisions regarding the spraying of chemicals into the skies above your head. You can speak up on whether construction quality control includes things like toxic paint. You can lobby the community to set up public walkways with fruit trees instead of planting a bunch of trees that do nothing.

Get involved. Be an activist.

Create the future as you want it to be, not in response to the broken system.

Be active in your community. Help community organic gardens. Use your skills to help with water delivery, or to help with air quality. Put your ideas out there. Share them with the world and contribute to your society. As an industry professional, whatever industry you are in, you are a part of this society, and you have the power to help change it.

There are so many possibilities once we make the decision to make a better society. Doors will open when we stop simply reacting and start giving in to the dream. It is amazing what you can do.

CHAPTER FIVE

The Future of Society

PLAN FOR THE FUTURE OR PLAN FOR THE PRESENT?

Imagine there are potholes in the street and we need a plan to address them.

Here are two possibilities:

1. We can plan to fill in the potholes.
2. We can plan to recondition the street completely.

The first choice demonstrates *planning for the present*, while *planning for the future* is illustrated by the second choice. Planning for the present is typically a reflex response to a condition, while planning for the future means that you are looking ahead to the possibilities; you are looking at what might happen, what you would do to promote desired results, and what you might do to prevent undesirable events. Both plans address the present emergency, but the second also plans for contingencies, for growth, cycles, and future technologies.

When you plan for the future, your mindset is different. If we return to a chess analogy, you are thinking eleven chess moves ahead instead of just one. As in chess, the more you can think ahead, the more likely you are to succeed.

The difference between planning for the present and planning for the future is similar to the difference between emergency medicine and preventative medicine. Planning for the future is all about *creation* and planning for the present is all about *reaction*.

So, what do you want to create?

What do you want for your world?

We forget that this is a society that people created. This is our game. Every aspect of it that is not borne out of nature is something that we made up. We become stuck in our creations, which means that we exist by simply reacting, forgetting that we have the power to change the whole board. We have the power to look toward the future and create something different and better.

Amazing things can happen with just this one thought: *What do I want in this world?*

We have the ability to take all the amazing lessons that we have learned and then put them right next to a whole different plan for the future, for health, and for monetary and social growth.

Making Decisions Based on Forward Thinking Rather Than Money Concerns

Many of our health decisions are based on planning for the present. When it comes to eating healthfully, you might say that you can't afford organic food, and you can't afford to shop at the local health food store. You might think that making your own healthy meals costs more in money or time. If you are not planning for the future, you might select fast food or another food choice that isn't high quality, making your decision based on a money concern. You are not really looking at what's possible disease-wise in the future. You are not considering how much disease will cost you in the future. You know you are not necessarily going to feel the negative effects in this moment, and so you are making a plan-for-the-present choice.

Let's say I choose that McDonald's meal. I am going to eat that meal because it is cheap right now, but I am not considering that making these choices means I am going to have diabetes in ten years. Diabetes is going to cost $500 to $1000 per month just to take care of my health. The fact that I'm not thinking about these concerns in the moment is going to cost me a great deal in the future.

Most of the decisions we make have unintended as well as intended consequences. And if we only concern our decisions with money as the reasoning behind them — and this is true for healthcare, infrastructure, and just about everything else societally — we are leaving behind all the possibilities that making a better decision could lead to in the future.

Let's be cheap today can cost us dearly later.

Those unintended consequences could be much more fruitful and profitable for us if we think forward.

Leaving Behind the Technology of the Past

We have been learning a lot about the neuroplasticity of the brain in recent years. Part of what makes us humans, the cream of the crop of species, is that we have this thing called adaptability. We can adapt to our circumstances and we can adapt fairly quickly. The negative side effect of having the human brain is that we like to hold on to things longer than they are useful to us, whether it is pain and trauma — or technology.

They are still laying down coaxial cable to get TV in some areas, and they are still using an outdated grid system for electrical grids, which may cause cancer problems and other health problems because of the electromagnetic field (EMF).

We know that the technology is old, and yet we have decided to keep it, instead of upgrading the infrastructure using better technology and leaving that old stuff behind. These shortsighted decisions are often based on money, but we also tend to be attached to our innovations. We must learn to be willing to say: *That was an awesome innovation for its time, and now, its time is done.*

If we can leave behind the old technology, we can get to what we have created for the future faster. Big companies are horrible at this because they do not have much adaptability. It takes a massive effort for them to move.

When we create new technologies with a future-thinking or forward-thinking mindset, we can also create tools that are more adaptable so that they are easy to replace and leave behind when new technologies are available. Planning like this will enable the next generation to move forward faster with better results. It is amazing what is possible when you can think ahead instead of thinking behind.

Hundred-Year Plan

Often when I listen to politicians talk about concerns about money, I hear them refer to ten- or twenty-year plans. So, they are making laws, plans, budgets that will be implemented over the next ten to twenty years. Is today's solution really going to work in ten to twenty years? Twenty years from now, we will have that *today solution,* and it will be outdated.

Instead, what if we think ahead one hundred years and contemplate *that* future?

Let's follow this train of thought:

- We think about what we want to create in the next hundred years.
- We think about where we are going instead of reacting to what is.
- We think about exactly what it is going to take to get there.
- With the answer to these questions, we backtrack all the way to the present and begin to build a hundred-year plan.

This is a standard operational plan kind of thinking that can enable us to create a society now that is designed for the future rather than designed for the past.

How many of us are still living in 1950s-style suburbia?

We are not living in *The Jetson's* age; we are not living in the age of *Terminator* or *Back to the Future;* we are still living in the past. New technology is so slow to reach us. If we can think a hundred years ahead and backtrack to now, we can start creating our future. We can start building the future in a way that is exciting and revolutionary as opposed to just patching *what is*.

We could be designing revolutionary new inventions instead of patching up the current problems. For example, it is a good idea to promote the use of non-toxic paint to replace toxic paint, but what if your new paint could actually provide ionic health benefits as well? What if that paint could create digital scenes? It is doable, and we are not doing it yet because we are not thinking a hundred years in the future.

What do we want our lives to be like then?

USING TECHNOLOGY TO BRING US BACK TO NATURE

In this industrial age, we learned how to harness nature to create computers, warehousing, engineering, and a means of mechanizing the world. We developed revolutionary and amazing technologies. Now it is the age of using that technology to bring us back toward nature, rather than creating smog, pollution, and a societal or natural deficit.

In agriculture, rather than stripping our soil of all its mineral content and over-using that natural resource of water, we can use hydroponics and aeroponics. We can use fish farms and other agricultural innovations to feed our world in a way that we were not able to do before. We can use technology to bring us back to nature. We can use technology to help clean up the environment, and to create societies that are deficit-neutral, that provide no harsh impact. We can add to the environment instead of taking away from the environment. It is pretty cool what is possible when we use our technology for good, so to speak.

Our nature is for growth. Everything in nature is about growth. And we have the ability to stifle that growth like no other species on earth. Other species live their nature; we attempt to control our nature.

We need to bring back the idea, the philosophy, that we are natural beings living in a natural world.

Like all of nature, we have this need and ambition to grow. We can use that ambition to grow in a better way. We can use technology to bring us back to ourselves, back to our nature. Rather than our growth pushing aside competition, perhaps we can focus on living in balance with the community.

How do we live in balance with our friends, family, and neighbors?

How do we create our society to be healthy, to be futuristic, and to be aligned with nature?

Communities to Support a Natural Lifestyle

This may sound a little odd, but we have designed our communities to revolve around commuting. We must drive places, we ride in our cars to go to the office, we drive our cars to come home, and then, we sit on the couch.

As we've discussed, we can design our communities in a natural way instead. If we created communities to support a natural lifestyle, we would design walking paths everywhere. Instead of having an extra oak tree that we plant for looks, we might plant orange trees and apple trees and fig trees and lemon trees so that anybody who is on their walk can grab a snack, a real fast food snack right off the tree.

We can create community gardens and a work environment to support movement and air and breath. Instead of stuffing people in cubicles, we can create open-air environments, places where people can stand and work and interact with each other.

A community that supports a natural lifestyle is all about movement and seeking knowledge, so it is lively and vibrant. There is less work and more play. We are not naturally designed to sit at a desk eight hours a day. We are designed to be moving and interacting and communicating with people.

We can design communities to reflect what we are designed to be and how we want to be. We can create a society to enhance those amazing attributes and leave behind some of the attributes that we do not like about our nature. We can literally design our future.

Investing in the Future

We keep wanting to put off things like replacing infrastructure because it costs so much. But we are not looking at the fact that in twenty years, costs are going to be higher, right? We are not looking at the fact that in the future, our technologies will be different, and this will make it more difficult to accomplish what we want.

We are doing much too little when it comes to investing in the future. Often, we are leaving technology on the table until the past technology pays for itself.

Let's say I am a medical office manager, and I bought an MRI machine costing ten million dollars. Two years later, I have only paid off about five million of that cost, but a new machine is out, and it has a diagnostic ability twenty times the machine I have.

Is my decision going to be based on keeping my past investment until it pays off?

Should I get the new machine and use it to get better results?

Better results can mean better business and more clients, so the second scenario is investing in the future. If we take the money that we think we don't have now, and we it put toward the possibilities, we will be investing in the future. We can create a better quality business using the new technology, the expenses that we currently have due to the present system will disappear, and the lifestyle that we create could be so much more amazing.

Let's start investing in the future of health care. People will get better and the costs will diminish in a huge way. That investment in health will be paid for in full.

Right now, we are thinking: *Well, we are not ready for that.*

Here is my plea. When you are thinking about what to invest in, when you are thinking about the money you have and do not have, ignore it all and go back toward these thoughts:

- *What is it that I want to create?*
- *What does the future hold?*
- *How can we create a healthy and vibrant future instead of a reactive reaction to the past?*

Purpose-Driven Communities

How can we move toward the future faster and more efficiently?

In raising a futuristic society, you could have what I call purpose-driven communities, focused on a particular goal or purpose. I love this idea. It differs vastly from the traditional hierarchy of the typical business structure.

When you go into a typical company building, you have all the accountants in one department, all the engineers in another department, with the leadership on another floor above everybody else. A hierarchy is apparent in the workings of the company.

However, some of the more modern companies are starting to create project-driven communities, in which the engineers are working with the accountants, with the customer service, with the delivery, and so on. Everyone is working on a project together.

From this project-driven structure, we can create purpose-driven communities. Suppose I am a person who wants clean water for the entire world. Other people who have that same goal could come in together to create a community where that is its goal. You have a goal-driven or purpose-driven community instead of several people working separately on their own islands.

Together, you can create from a place of ambition and creativity rather than from a place of reaction. I keep going back to that same idea, don't I? Futuristic societies could be purpose-driven societies, societies that are meant for something, that have a reason for being, that are vibrant, lively, happy, together societies. There would be less violence. There would be less crime.

These kinds of societies could create the future in a way that is at ease. Their tone is relaxed and cooperative. This is so much better than having an idea, sitting in your basement, and working on it alone.

If we can raise our societies as purpose-driven, then we can create a world that we really enjoy. We can create community organizations made up of a diverse set of people who know how to collaborate and use each other for the benefit of all. Using purpose-driven communities, we can build this kind of futuristic, utopian society. And that is what I would love to see our future become.

THE POWER OF CHANGE

Change is inevitable. It is its own power. There is nothing that we can do to stop change because change will stop us. We will end up dying and change will still happen. There is nothing we can do to stop things from changing. However, that doesn't mean that we have no control over change.

We have some choices when it comes to change:

- We can go with it or we can fight it.
- We can stifle it or we can enhance it.
- We can direct it.
- We can create from it.

The power of change is that when we embrace it, we create from that place. When we fight change, we create from *that* place. What I want to get across is although the power of change is inevitable, the pleasure of being human is the allowance and the direction of that change. We know change is inevitable, but when we take control of it, we can direct that change instead of being a victim of that change.

It does not matter who you want to be and what kind of society you want to live in, the power of change first starts in your mindset. First, you must be aware that *what is* right now is not all that is possible. Your current situation is alterable, transformable. And when you come to that conclusion, where you live no longer is a factor because you can always move. What you currently know is no longer a factor because you can always change and transform.

What our society looks like currently is no longer a factor because we can create it the way we want it. We made it up to begin with. We can turn it into a game, or we can create it all over again. We can make something new that works better, is more effective, and brings us together in a way that people only dream of.

And that works because mindset powers change.

Excitement

Excitement can physiologically act in many different ways. It can appear as something different, like fear or anxiety. Excitement, anxiety, and fear all produce the same chemistry in your body. If you can change the way you think, transforming fear of the unknown to excitement of what is possible, then we have something to work with. Excitement about what is possible can drive creativity.

When you have the ability to think outside the box, you can put this thought in your mind: *I can change what I see.*

You now have the ability to ask: *What changes will improve this situation? What can I transform in order to create something new?*

That is exciting. And that excitement is energy. That energy creates manifestation. Manifestation creates what you are wanting to create or change. When we are scared and fearful, we can alter those feelings and transform them into excitement. Then we can take that excitement and use it to incite movement through change.

That is the power. The power is in you. And the power is in us as a society. And when we get excited about the possibility of change and excited about what can be, we can do something amazing.

We hear politicians talking about how they wish they could go back to how it was, right?

What is cool is that we can, in some ways. We can take the best parts of what was, the best parts of what we have, and the best parts of what we can imagine, and put them together to create the future with excitement.

Momentum

An object at rest tends to stay at rest, and an object in motion tends to stay in motion. Momentum is motion at accelerating speeds. Let's think about that for a second. If momentum is motion at accelerating speed, you can envision something like a snowball going down a mountain.

It starts small and ends up getting bigger, bigger, bigger, right?

As you start developing your creative edge on how to make this society better and work more for the future, as we do that collectively, we also create this thing called momentum. As we work on the future, more possibilities will keep popping up, expanding outward, increasing speed and drive exponentially. This is what it's like to work from a place of creation and momentum. If, instead, we were working from a place of struggle and fight instead, we would feel like it might take ten years.

Your momentum and your excitement will draw in more people, more resources, more teams, more ideas, etc. And that will drive the next process and the next, into the future. What is possible becomes exponentially grander when momentum draws in more people.

Think of Gandhi as an example. He started his Dandi March, and millions followed with acts of civil disobedience. He created momentum from his excitement about the possibility of change. Kind of cool, huh?

What Is Possible?

What is possible?

Instead, let's ask: *What is not possible?*

That is my question. What is not possible? Can you think of anything that is not possible? At all? Zero possibility?

When you come from the position that everything is possible, then everything *is* possible. You have excitement and momentum. You have your ideas, your creativity, and the power of change. From all of this, *what is possible* becomes *what is*.

What is possible becomes what is because you are in momentum; you are in motion. You have the motion of energy going forward, and that excitement will draw in the universe to conspire, to create what you have envisioned.

So, take a deep breath, realize that the power of what is possible is limited only by what we believe. Take your fear and your worry and your anxiety, transform them into excitement, create momentum, and what is possible will show up, every single time.

That is the universal law. I challenge you to test me. Create what is possible. Let's see if what I am saying is true.

Did you hear me?

Conclusion

Mindset is where we started. Mindset is where everything starts. Everything that is in our physical world started in our minds. Every chair that you sit in, every TV show that you watch started in somebody's mind. Everything began with a mindset.

One thing that I have realized is that we, as a society, deliver a lot of hope and possibility. But we don't foster *faith*.

We tell people: *Hope for the best and expect the worst,* and that becomes our mindset.

Change your mindset! Foster faith. If I can leave you with one thought, it would be to have faith.

Do you think about creating something better in the future?

Have faith you can do that. Believe that those things are doable rather than just hoping things may someday get better.

With that mindset, you will become a leader who generates the momentum to create the future. In order to do that, you will need to think critically about things. You will need to take big ideas and break them down into smaller chunks so they do not overwhelm you. Mindset is really about believing at your core that the things that intrigue you and make you passionate about living are the things that you are meant to do.

Here is one final piece of advice: *Start now*.

Even if it is little steps, even if it is with the limited resources that you have, start now living your passionate purpose. Take an inventory of who you are and become active. Activate yourself; energize yourself to create the future. And that small step will begin creating momentum to create the future of society.

Everything is possible. Think about the consequences — beyond the consequences — and beyond those consequences — of your actions and create the future you want. Get involved in your community. Get involved with your neighbors. Get involved with your passions. Live a life filled with purpose and meaning so that you can truly make a difference.

You already do.

Next Steps

After reading this book, have you written down your ideas and inspirations?

Have you created an action plan?

Are you ready to move your personal transformation forward?

Do you need some help getting started?

It is all about you, not a technique or specific modality, but a channeled, guided journey into you.

Feel free to contact Ari Gronich at:

Email: info@achievehealthusa.com

Phone: (321) 541-0FIT (0348)

Website: www.AchieveHealthUSA.com

Ari is available for interviews, speaking engagements, and educational opportunities, as well as mentoring, coaching, and consulting.

About the Author

Ari Gronich is known as *The Performance Therapist*. He has become the go-to guy for sports and accident injury rehabilitation and prevention. He is the founder and CEO of Achieve Health USA, LLC and is the lead instructor and founder of the Performance Therapy Academy. He has served on the advisory boards of several health and wellness nonprofit organizations.

Ari has been highly trained in many disciplines within the fields of bodywork, kinesiology, nutrition, health, and sports therapy. He has over 25,000 hours of hands-on work and 5,000+ plus hours of training and internship. Ari has trained hundreds of other therapists in the field.

Working with world-class athletes has given him a unique perspective in taking an athlete from amateur to professional and giving these athletes longevity in their careers through prevention and rehabilitation of injury. He brings these skills to help everyone that comes to him live a more pain-free and injury-free life!

Ari is a life-long learner. He has attended a multitude of life-transforming workshops since childhood. He practiced Buddhism alongside going to temple studying for his Bar Mitzvah, and then his inquiring mind brought him to studying other religions, philosophies, and spiritual paths.

Ari has presented workshops with Mark Victor Hansen, author of *Chicken Soup for the Soul*; Robert Allen, author of *One Minute Millionaire* and a founder of The Enlightened Wealth Institute; Clinton Swaine of Frontier Games; Berny Dohrmann from CEO Space International; Adam Markel from Peak Potentials; The Medical Fitness Association; Achieve Systems; and many more.

Ari has helped transform his clients' bodies and lives through increased flexibility, performance, and power, enhancing physical as well as mental and emotional health. Through his work with Achieve Health USA and the Performance Therapy Academy,

A New Tomorrow

he educates other doctors, therapists, and trainers to become the best they can be, while at the same time, brings a wellness and productivity to businesses nationwide through individualized corporate programs designed to increase the vitality and health of the workplace.

Ari brings love, experience, strength, and compassion to his work as a healer. He brings a sense of peace and understanding. Ari utilizes styles from all over the world and combines them in a unique way that is solely about healing.

As a philanthropist, Ari has always been cause-driven. He seeks to help create a balanced society where we take care of not only the business side of life, but also the health of our citizens in body, mind, and spirit.

www.ingramcontent.com/pod-product-compliance
Lightning Source LLC
Chambersburg PA
CBHW072157160426
43197CB00012B/2420